Try Not To

LAUGH

Leprechaun Endorsed!

Joke Book

Challenge

Saint Patrick's Day Edition

Try Not To Laugh Game Rules

Easy Version

1. Find an opponent or split up into two teams.
2. Team 1 reads a joke to Team 2 from anywhere in the book.
3. The person reading the joke looks right at the opposing person or team and can use silly voices and funny faces if they wish.
4. If Team 2:

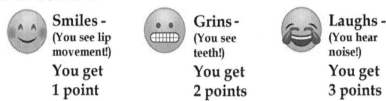

Smiles - (You see lip movement!) You get 1 point	Grins - (You see teeth!) You get 2 points	Laughs - (You hear noise!) You get 3 points

5. Read one joke at at time, then switch the giving and receiving teams.
6. The team with most points after five rounds wins! Use the score sheets on the following pages.

Challenge Version

1. Same rules apply except you get one point if you can make the other team laugh. No points for smiling or grinning.

Good luck and try not to laugh!

SCORE SHEET

	TEAM 1	TEAM 2
ROUND 1		
ROUND 2		
ROUND 3		
ROUND 4		
ROUND 5		
TOTAL		

	TEAM 1	TEAM 2
ROUND 1		
ROUND 2		
ROUND 3		
ROUND 4		
ROUND 5		
TOTAL		

	TEAM 1	TEAM 2
ROUND 1		
ROUND 2		
ROUND 3		
ROUND 4		
ROUND 5		
TOTAL		

	TEAM 1	TEAM 2
ROUND 1		
ROUND 2		
ROUND 3		
ROUND 4		
ROUND 5		
TOTAL		

	TEAM 1	TEAM 2
ROUND 1		
ROUND 2		
ROUND 3		
ROUND 4		
ROUND 5		
TOTAL		

	TEAM 1	TEAM 2
ROUND 1		
ROUND 2		
ROUND 3		
ROUND 4		
ROUND 5		
TOTAL		

	TEAM 1	TEAM 2
ROUND 1		
ROUND 2		
ROUND 3		
ROUND 4		
ROUND 5		
TOTAL		

	TEAM 1	TEAM 2
ROUND 1		
ROUND 2		
ROUND 3		
ROUND 4		
ROUND 5		
TOTAL		

SCORE SHEET

	TEAM 1	TEAM 2
ROUND 1		
ROUND 2		
ROUND 3		
ROUND 4		
ROUND 5		
TOTAL		

	TEAM 1	TEAM 2
ROUND 1		
ROUND 2		
ROUND 3		
ROUND 4		
ROUND 5		
TOTAL		

	TEAM 1	TEAM 2
ROUND 1		
ROUND 2		
ROUND 3		
ROUND 4		
ROUND 5		
TOTAL		

	TEAM 1	TEAM 2
ROUND 1		
ROUND 2		
ROUND 3		
ROUND 4		
ROUND 5		
TOTAL		

	TEAM 1	TEAM 2
ROUND 1		
ROUND 2		
ROUND 3		
ROUND 4		
ROUND 5		
TOTAL		

	TEAM 1	TEAM 2
ROUND 1		
ROUND 2		
ROUND 3		
ROUND 4		
ROUND 5		
TOTAL		

	TEAM 1	TEAM 2
ROUND 1		
ROUND 2		
ROUND 3		
ROUND 4		
ROUND 5		
TOTAL		

	TEAM 1	TEAM 2
ROUND 1		
ROUND 2		
ROUND 3		
ROUND 4		
ROUND 5		
TOTAL		

SCORE SHEET

	TEAM 1	TEAM 2
ROUND 1		
ROUND 2		
ROUND 3		
ROUND 4		
ROUND 5		
TOTAL		

	TEAM 1	TEAM 2
ROUND 1		
ROUND 2		
ROUND 3		
ROUND 4		
ROUND 5		
TOTAL		

	TEAM 1	TEAM 2
ROUND 1		
ROUND 2		
ROUND 3		
ROUND 4		
ROUND 5		
TOTAL		

	TEAM 1	TEAM 2
ROUND 1		
ROUND 2		
ROUND 3		
ROUND 4		
ROUND 5		
TOTAL		

	TEAM 1	TEAM 2
ROUND 1		
ROUND 2		
ROUND 3		
ROUND 4		
ROUND 5		
TOTAL		

	TEAM 1	TEAM 2
ROUND 1		
ROUND 2		
ROUND 3		
ROUND 4		
ROUND 5		
TOTAL		

	TEAM 1	TEAM 2
ROUND 1		
ROUND 2		
ROUND 3		
ROUND 4		
ROUND 5		
TOTAL		

	TEAM 1	TEAM 2
ROUND 1		
ROUND 2		
ROUND 3		
ROUND 4		
ROUND 5		
TOTAL		

SCORE SHEET

	TEAM 1	TEAM 2
ROUND 1		
ROUND 2		
ROUND 3		
ROUND 4		
ROUND 5		
TOTAL		

	TEAM 1	TEAM 2
ROUND 1		
ROUND 2		
ROUND 3		
ROUND 4		
ROUND 5		
TOTAL		

	TEAM 1	TEAM 2
ROUND 1		
ROUND 2		
ROUND 3		
ROUND 4		
ROUND 5		
TOTAL		

	TEAM 1	TEAM 2
ROUND 1		
ROUND 2		
ROUND 3		
ROUND 4		
ROUND 5		
TOTAL		

	TEAM 1	TEAM 2
ROUND 1		
ROUND 2		
ROUND 3		
ROUND 4		
ROUND 5		
TOTAL		

	TEAM 1	TEAM 2
ROUND 1		
ROUND 2		
ROUND 3		
ROUND 4		
ROUND 5		
TOTAL		

	TEAM 1	TEAM 2
ROUND 1		
ROUND 2		
ROUND 3		
ROUND 4		
ROUND 5		
TOTAL		

	TEAM 1	TEAM 2
ROUND 1		
ROUND 2		
ROUND 3		
ROUND 4		
ROUND 5		
TOTAL		

SCORE SHEET

	TEAM 1	TEAM 2
ROUND 1		
ROUND 2		
ROUND 3		
ROUND 4		
ROUND 5		
TOTAL		

	TEAM 1	TEAM 2
ROUND 1		
ROUND 2		
ROUND 3		
ROUND 4		
ROUND 5		
TOTAL		

	TEAM 1	TEAM 2
ROUND 1		
ROUND 2		
ROUND 3		
ROUND 4		
ROUND 5		
TOTAL		

	TEAM 1	TEAM 2
ROUND 1		
ROUND 2		
ROUND 3		
ROUND 4		
ROUND 5		
TOTAL		

	TEAM 1	TEAM 2
ROUND 1		
ROUND 2		
ROUND 3		
ROUND 4		
ROUND 5		
TOTAL		

	TEAM 1	TEAM 2
ROUND 1		
ROUND 2		
ROUND 3		
ROUND 4		
ROUND 5		
TOTAL		

	TEAM 1	TEAM 2
ROUND 1		
ROUND 2		
ROUND 3		
ROUND 4		
ROUND 5		
TOTAL		

	TEAM 1	TEAM 2
ROUND 1		
ROUND 2		
ROUND 3		
ROUND 4		
ROUND 5		
TOTAL		

Why did the Irish sheep
turn around?
**She needed to make a
ewe turn!**

Why are leprechauns so
hard to get along with?
**Because they're very
short-tempered!**

Where would you find a leprechaun baseball team?
In the Little League!

How do you know when an Irishman is tired of your story?
He lets out a lepre-yawn.

Did you hear about the Irish girl who failed her coloring test?
She needed a shoulder to crayon.

What happened when the Irishman's flashlight batteries died?
He was delighted.

What is an Irish
lumberjack's most favorite
part about his computer?
Logging in.

Why did the Irishman
stand on the clock?
**He really wanted
to be on time.**

What type of bow
cannot be tied?
A rainbow.

What do you call a
leprechaun's vacation
home?
A lepre-condo.

What is it called when you do the wrong Irish dance?
A jig mistake!

What are Irish rivers so rich?
They have two banks.

What happened when the Irishman wanted to retire from being a traffic cop?
His boss gave him the green light.

How did the leprechaun get to the moon?
By shamrocket.

What do you call leprechauns who collect cans and plastic?
Wee-cyclers.

Knock knock.
Who's there?
Dawn.
Dawn who?
Dawn't be putting down the Irish now, ya hear!

How did the leprechaun win Olympic Gold in cycling?
He put the pedal to the medal.

ST.
PATRICK'S
DAY

Why did the Irishman's vision start improving?
The luck of the iris.

Why did Saint Patrick
drive all the snakes
out of Ireland?
**He couldn't afford
the airfare!**

What do you call a
bald Irish zombie?
A lock-less monster.

How does an Irishman
know he's sick with kell?
He has kell tics.

What did the leprechaun
referee say when the
soccer match ended?
"Game clover."

What are so many
leprechauns florists?
**Because they have
green thumbs.**

What is an Irishman's
favorite subject in school?
Jigonometry!

What happens when a
leprechaun falls into
a river?
He gets wet.

Why was the leprechaun
doing the Irish jig in
a McDonald's?
**He heard the customers
loved Shamrock shakes.**

What do you call a fake
Irish stone?
A shamrock.

What baseball position do
leprechauns usually play?
Shortstop.

Did you hear about the first Irishman to grill hamburgers?
He got a paddy on the back.

What do you call a leprechaun who disappears?
A lepre-gone!

What did the Irishman say after trying sweet potatoes?
"Boy, I yam happy!"

Why did the Irishman quit his job at the doughnut factory?
He was fed up with the hole business.

Why did the Irish cook
spill his soup?
**Because there was a
leek in the pot.**

What would you get if you
crossed a leprechaun with
a Texan?
**A pot of chili at the
end of the rainbow.**

How did the leprechaun
beat the boy to the
pot of gold?
He took a shortcut!

What happened when the
Irishman tries to play
the bagpipes?
**The sound was
off kilter.**

Why shouldn't your iron a four-leaf clover?
You'll press your luck!

Why did the Irishman only exercise on Saturdays and Sundays?
Because the rest are weak days.

Why do you call a
complaining leprechaun at
a company where they dig
for gold?
A miner problem.

What do you get when two
leprechauns have a
conversation?
A lot of small talk.

Who was St. Patrick's favorite superhero?
Green Lantern.

Why did the leprechaun stand on the potato?
To keep from falling into the stew.

Why couldn't the Irishman
make a boat out of stone?
**Because it would have
been too much of a
hardship.**

What do you call a
leprechaun with a sore
throat?
A streprechuan!

Knock knock.
Who's there?
Irish.
Irish who?
Irish I were an Oscar Mayer wiener!

Why is Ireland like a wine bottle?
Because it has a Cork in it!

What do you call a lucky dog?
A four-leaf rover.

What did one shamrock say to the other shamrock when it saw St. Patrick across the field?
"Look clover there."

Why do people wear
shamrocks on Saint
Patrick's Day?
**Because regular rocks
are too heavy!**

Did the Irishman like
being a vegetarian?
**No, it was a
missed steak.**

What was the Irish
shepherd late?
**He had a staff
meeting.**

What is a leprechaun's
favorite type of music?
Shamrock and roll!

Did you hear about the leprechaun who collected candy canes? **They were all in mint condition.**

What is a leprechaun's favorite cereal? **Lucky Charms!**

What are Irish fishermen
always searching for?
Clamrocks.

What's big and purple and
lies next to Ireland?
Grape Britain.

Why did Cole want his
cabbage served cold?
**Because it was
Cole's law.**

Why don't Irish people like
long fairytales?
**Because they tend
to dragon.**

Where do leprechauns
sit to relax?
**Shamrocking
chairs.**

What did the Irish laundry
man go searching for?
**The fold at the end
of the rainbow.**

What do you call a small Irishman used as a chess piece?
A lepre-pawn.

Does the Irish Terrier have a lot of potential?
Yes, he just needs to unleash it.

What does a leprechaun
call a happy man
wearing green?
A Jolly Green Giant.

Why don't Irish people
play hockey?
**The can never find the
puck of the Irish.**

Why did the Irish singer stand on the chair?
So she could reach the high notes.

What happened when the Irishman went to Texas?
He started the wearing' of the jean.

I made a new friend in Ireland.
You might say,
"Oh, really?"
But it was an O'Reilly.

Why was the old Irish priest sent to another church?
The parishioners were looking for greener pastors.

Did you hear about the
Irish nun who didn't
do her laundry?
**She had a filthy
habit.**

What did the Irish potato
say to his girlfriend?
**"I only have eyes
for you!"**

What do you call an Irish lad being carried around by another Irish lad?
A Pat on the back.

What don't Irish people ever hit their heads?
The duck of the Irish.

What did the Irish cheese find at the end of the rainbow?
A pot of mold!

What is the difference between a nicely dressed Irishman on a tricycle and a poorly dressed Irishman on a bicycle?
A tire.

Do leprechauns make good secretaries?
Sure, they are great at shorthand.

When is an Irish potato not an Irish potato?
When it's a French fry.

Did you hear about the leprechaun who worked at the diner?
He was a short-order cook.

What do you call a small Irishman who always agrees with you?
A yep-rechaun!

Knock knock.
Who's there?
Irish stew.
Irish stew who?
Irish stew you in the name of the law.

What do you call an Irishman who keeps bouncing off the walls?
Rick O'Shea.

What do you call Irish
timepieces that are
always wrong?
Sham clocks.

What did the leprechaun
order to drink at the
Chinese restaurant?
Green tea.

What was the Irish
lamb cold?
**He lost his
muttons.**

Knock knock.
Who's there?
Pat.
Pat who?
**Pat your coat on and
let's go find some gold!**

What do you call an Irish spider?
Paddy long legs.

How can you tell if an Irishman finds your joke funny?
He's Dublin over with laughter.

What happened to the Irish fisherman who was going to tell a joke?
He forgot the line.

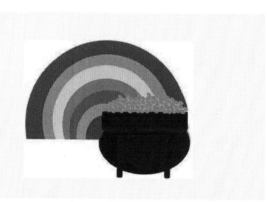

What happened when the Irish pilot, taking his flying test, flew through a rainbow?
He passed with flying colors.

What Stone Age cartoon character loves St. Patrick's Day?
Blarney Rubble.

Good Luck

How do you know if someone is jealous of an Irish person?
They are green with envy.

What do you call a
leprechaun who can see
the future and just
escaped from jail?
**A small medium
at large.**

What is there not a
Balloon family in Ireland?
It ran out of heir.

Why do leprechauns recycle?
They like to go green!

Knock knock.
Who's there?
Aaron.
Aaron who?
Aaron go bragh and all that Irish talk!

What did one Irish ghost
say to the other
Irish ghost?
**"Top o' the moanin'
to you!"**

What do you get when you
fall into a patch of four-leaf
clovers and poison ivy?
A rash of bad luck!

What do you call a performance by a leprechaun band?
A lepre-concert.

Knock, knock.
Who's there?
Saint.
Saint who?
Saint no time for questions, open the door!

What do leprechauns
love to barbecue?
Short ribs.

Did you hear about the
Irish magician who
loved chocolate?
**He could perform
a lot of Twix.**

Thanks for reading!
Check out our other
Try Not To Laugh
books as well!

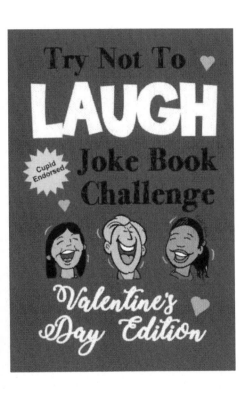

Made in the USA
Columbia, SC
09 March 2020